Coming Out

"I Think I'm Gay"

*The Ultimate Guide
to Self-Acceptance,
Coming Out, Building
a Support System, and
Loving Your New Life*

by Kevin Brison

Table of Contents

Introduction..1

Chapter 1: What is Gay, Anyway?...................7

Chapter 2: Coming Out of the Closet........................15

Chapter 3: Establishing Positive Reinforcement.......21

Chapter 4: Rebirth as Your True Self..........................31

Chapter 5: Ten Things to Remember.........................37

Conclusion...45

Introduction

I want to thank you and congratulate you for purchasing the book, "I Think I'm Gay: The Ultimate Guide to Self-Acceptance, Coming Out, Building a Support System, and Loving Your New Life."

This book contains proven steps and strategies on how to let out that person you are, instead of the person others think you are, or the person you think you should be. Take note: the title starts with an uncertain statement "I think I'm gay". This is your starting line. Don't be too hasty to make a determination. In truth, sexuality has a lot of gray areas, and there is a tendency to want to label yourself to the point that it makes you do things you don't want to do or be someone closer to who you want to be, but not exactly.

This book will be divided into several chapters. Each chapter is designed to bring you closer to your goal of finding yourself, being comfortable in your own skin, finding acceptance, a support system, and personal growth.

This book will not tell you to do what you want, regardless of what it is. Rather, it advocates responsibility which goes hand in hand with your personal identity. To paraphrase a popular anecdote: "Your right to individuality and freedom starts from within. This right ends the moment you become a hazard to yourself and to others".

This book will not tell you how to live life as a gay person. It centers more on living the life you were meant to live—free from unwarranted judgment from others and from yourself.

The word "gay" is more associated with men who are attracted to men. Women who are attracted to women are better known as lesbians. However, the principles provided in this book are applicable to both. It also applies to bisexuals and transgenders.

This book is not a scientific treatise not is it a scholarly work. It is a summation of experience by the author. The same is being shared in order to help you in your transition.

Thanks again for purchasing this book, I hope you enjoy it!

Chapter 1: What is Gay, Anyway?

Half a century ago, the basic dictionary definition of the word "gay", meant to be happy. A decade ago, the word "gay" was a derogatory word that connotes unacceptable, effeminate behavior in males. Nowadays, the stigma has subsided. The word "gay" is more identified as a word that signifies a person who is attracted to the same sex as he/she is. More specifically, it applies to a male person who is attracted physically and emotionally to another male. Let us start from there.

What Does This Tell You?

Simply put, people have begun to socially accept gays (and lesbians). Think about it: words follow actions. Because people have started accepting the gay community, then the word and its accepted meaning have also changed from derogatory to a fact of life that is entirely acceptable.

The Gay Gene?

Most experts agree that being gay depends on several factors. This includes but is not limited to genetics, biology, your environment while growing up, psychology, specific events, and peer interaction. It even occurs in nature, for example different species i.e. birds, mammals, marine life, etc. Most important to understand, being gay is certainly not a sickness, nor can it be "cured".

Being Gay

A gay person is more than just someone who is attracted to other men. It isn't a lifestyle choice. Nor is it a passing fancy. Being gay is an identity that you were born with and must accept. In doing so, you will avoid conflicts and confusion later on in life. Put simply, if you are gay, then you need to BE GAY. Those who do not accept this side of themselves are somewhere in between which is a very confusing place, and may cause emotional pain and trauma.

Gay Men and Homophobia

You would be surprised to find out that even gay men have to deal with their OWN homophobia. This is before they deal with how others view and treat them. Are you afraid, or sometimes even appalled at your own feelings, thoughts, and actions?

Well don't be afraid; these feelings are only natural. Even openly gay men have to deal with homophobia. Case in point is Neil Patrick Harris. He was once interviewed on how different playing Barney Stinson (How I Met Your Mother) is from his new role in "Hedwig and the Angry Inch". He told the reporter that, even as an openly gay man, he was still uncomfortable with certain acts associated (but not monopolized) with being gay i.e. cross dressing, promiscuity, excess drama, etc.

He had to accept the fact that he was not this type of gay person. Or rather, he was not this type of person. Others are, but he is not. In the end, by opening himself to this reality, it helped him affirm his identity.

Trying to Be Heterosexual

In some cases, gay men try to fit into the shoes of a heterosexual person. You might be the same too. You simplify things as right or wrong, and you use the measuring stick that you were born and raised with, and the one that society has historically imposed. All that hiding, denial, and self-loathing will warp the way you think about your identity.

Worst case scenario is you blame your being gay for your miserable life. I have actually experienced this myself. In fact, it's a recurring reaction that gets dragged to the surface because of some act or omission on the part of other less tolerant individuals. The key to moving past this is twofold. First, you need to accept yourself. No matter what type of gay person you are. Second, you need to stop minding what other less tolerant segments of society might think of you. Focus on those who accept you for who you are! Of course, self acceptance presupposes you are a responsible good-natured person that is worthy of acceptance.

Moving Beyond the Stereotype

The popular misconception is that a gay man dresses like a drag queen, is loud, effeminate, and frequents gay bars, singing YMCA. Granted, some gay men prefer to dress and act this way. But this is only a personal choice and self expression. This is not what awaits a gay person once he comes out of the closet. Simply put, like any human being, you have the right to dress the way you want as long as it is not inherently offensive.

The key word is "inherently" which connotes some form of universal un-acceptance. And even this is determined by where you are. For example, obviously it is not acceptable to wear a skimpy 2 piece bikini inside a place of religious worship. But a gay person who chooses to wear the same 2 piece may go unnoticed in a western country, especially within a state where openly gay relationships are accepted.

Unfocused Attraction during Puberty

I realized there was something different about myself, pre puberty. During puberty, all sorts of feelings became jumbled. Attraction to men, women, ideas, etc., just emerged, seemingly without cause. So don't worry, it's not only you. Simply put; it's puberty and your body that are making your emotions unstable. Once you get past the awkward puberty phase, attraction should become more focused and your actual desires more clear.

The Bottom Line

Every gay person is different. Just like any heterosexual person. The keys to happiness really are:

- Admitting to your sexual, mental, emotional, psychological preference

- Defining yourself as a person (not as a 'type')

- Setting your freedom and boundaries

- Living a full and fulfilling life

Chapter 2: Coming Out of the Closet

The last chapter dealt with defining yourself and accepting yourself. This chapter will deal with transitioning yourself and the people around you into identifying and accepting your true self. Take note, all you really need to concentrate on is how you should let the people around you, especially the peopled closest to you, know you are gay. It is up to them whether they accept you or not.

A Personal Decision

First and foremost, "coming out" is a personal decision, and so is not coming out. Personally, I decided to make a celebration of the event. It's like a confirmation of sorts where you finally say to the world, "I am Gay". Personally speaking, it's much simpler to just go ahead and come out instead of having to deal with other people tip-toeing on the subject matter when you are around.

Beta Test

Social media is not the way to come out. At best, you can come out in your Facebook, Twitter, Instagram account, etc., after you've done so in person, with family and friends. In fact, it would be better to choose a couple of your closest relatives and friends first. By having a "soft opening", you are able to transition more smoothly. Best case scenario, when you do come out to all your friends, in social media, and to everyone else, you know that someone has your back!

Be Realistic

Some people will accept you for the way you are, but there are some people who will not. Some will not celebrate with you because homosexuality is against their belief system i.e. religion. Some are just plain homophobic. Realistically speaking, some of your friends may need time to fully accept you the way you are. This is especially true if you showed no signs of being gay; case and point is Ricky Martin. The best you can do is be thankful for those who embrace your true self; realize that some will not be as easy to sway as others; and accept the fact that some people will never fully understand. No biggie, coming out is a personal choice and personal affirmation. You must absolutely realize that any reluctance to support you by others has more to do with THEIR issues than YOURS. Let it be their problem, and move forward with your life. You should actually feel sorry for those people because they hearts and minds are closed instead of open; what a pity. For them. But not you.

Timing is Key

Coming out can be simple or complicated depending on your personal situation. For example, maybe you're concerned your parents won't accept you the way you are; or your employer has something against gay people; or you live in a small tightly knit community and you are the first to come out, etc.

For some people, there is also the very real threat that you could get disowned. This is a very big problem, particularly if you are still a minor and/or your education is being paid by your parents. Be realistic here, even consider finishing your education first. But if you really insist on coming out now, it is best to find a way to emancipate yourself through a sufficient part time job and/or a place to stay for the long term. The best you can do, in the above mentioned situation, is to throw vague hints here and there and see how your parents and/or family members react.

Professional Advice

There are plenty of resources available to guide you along if you have questions, or just offer support when you may need it most. How about calling the hotline of Parents and Friends of Lesbians and Gays (PFLAG)? You can also visit their website, of course.

Just type the appropriate search word. This is a confidential yet informative way to get information on how to come out.

Question and Answer Portion

Well, you did it, you're out! It wasn't nearly as bad or as big of a deal as you were anticipating, was it? The next step is to be prepared for the barrage of questions and opinions you will get. Below are a few frequently asked questions. You should at least think about how you may want to answer them. Tip: when in doubt, just be honest.

- When did you realize you were gay?

- Are you attracted to men only or both men and women?

- Do you plan on having kids?

- Do you plan on marrying?

- Are you currently dating?

- Have you ever kissed or been with a person of the opposite sex?

- Are you sure you are not just confused?

- Are you sure this is what you want?

- Are you going to change the way you clothe yourself now?

- How did your parents take it? How about your family?

- What's next for you, now that you're out?

- Are you top or bottom? (This question refers to your sexual preference as a gay person. It is best not to answer this question because it steps over the line of your privacy).

Chapter 3: Establishing Positive Reinforcement

Every person draws strength from oneself and from others. This is no different for a gay person. Granted, you might find more reluctance, and rejection. The trick is to get your strength from the people who love you and brush off any other negativity that forces its way into your life.

Everything Starts with Family

If you are lucky enough, all your family members will accept your true self. Realistically speaking, if not everyone approves, all you can do is keep trying. By no means should it be a 24/7 active effort. Be yourself, and prove to them that you are still the same useful member of society that you always have been, and hope that in time, they will accept you. If not, be content with the fact that you have the support of some. And that you are finally living your life the way you want, to the fullest, and doing so responsibly. Tip: As mentioned earlier, start with the family member who is most understanding and can give you feedback/perspective on how to break the news, and how the others will take it. By confiding in your family, you give them the opportunity to accept you.

Stress how important it is that they know you, and if possible, accept you.

Your Relatives

Next to your immediate family members are your relatives. Statistically speaking, you might not get the support of all of them. This is because of the sheer number of relatives, lower your chances of full acceptance. Be prepared for this. Again. The best you can hope for is a slow acceptance process. Tip: don't show them too much too soon. Let them acclimate to your true self. For example, you may want to go out of the closet in stages.

- Stage 1: I'm gay

- Stage 2: He's my boyfriend

- Stage 3: We live together

- Stage 4: Marriage and Adoption

By doing this in stages and letting your family members know of your plans, you are inviting them into your life. Ultimately, what they care about is being a part of your life, loving you, and being loved by you. So if you shut them out, you are only setting the stage to make their acceptance even harder.

Close Friends

Based on my experience, friends are easier to break the news to. This is because, for some reason most individuals are more open to their friends and spend more time with them. Friends also are less likely to turn a blind eye and stick to a preconceived notion of you, as opposed to the "vibes" you are showing/giving off.

Co-Workers

Aim for a minimum work environment of mutual respect. This can be done by acting professionally and diligently. Realistically speaking, you will have to prove yourself again, now that you are out. Think of yourself as an ambassador for gay people out there. This is because, whether you like it or not, you are the "gay co-worker". Since this is now your role, do it with pride and represent them well. Tip: follow the rules but never hesitate to assert yourself as a worker and as a human being.

At School

If you are still studying, then coming out can either liberate you and let you move more naturally, or it can lead to bullying. In case of the latter, stand your ground, but don't stick out like a sore thumb. Tip: bullies like it when you react and overreact. Keep calm. Ignoring bullies often works. But if they persist, then consider reporting them to school authorities.

Social Media

Nowadays social media plays an important role in your support system. The likes, shares, favorites, etc. you get either builds or destroys your self esteem. The best way to get a positive atmosphere is to only friend those whom you really know. They don't have to approve of you as a gay person, but you have to know them and are sure that they are fair and responsible. Try not to put a target on your back as well by making sure to tweak your settings so only those groups you want to get certain updates get them. This is not censorship, but rather responsible social media etiquette.

Levels of Support

There are several levels of a support system. It can be as simple, as just knowing deep down inside that they have your back. It can be a more concrete gesture of affection i.e. text messages, calls, family get togethers, etc. Tip: don't wait for them to initiate contact. Play an active role i.e. plan weekly, bi-weekly or monthly get togethers; call them up during weekends for a chat; ask small favors you don't really need, etc.

It Goes Both Ways

Support goes both ways. You shouldn't always be the taker, otherwise you'll be branded a clingy, drama queen. Remember, not every little things requires you to go to pieces and break down. There are some things you want to keep to yourself. The trick is to know when you really, really need that helping hand. Always keep in mind that these people you're asking for support from have their own lives too. They have their own worries, troubles, and work that needs to be done. If you want them to be there for you in your time of need, then show them that you're there for them too. Just because you've decided to come out doesn't mean the world revolves around you now.

A Licensed Professional

Worst comes to worst, you want to have someone to call, a psychiatrist or a help hotline. Ask for referrals from other members of the gay community. At the very least, you can go to the PFLAG website for information and support.

Your Doctor

Let's get this out in the open; being gay carries with it certain risks that are higher than heterosexual relationships. The statistics are there. Even if you don't believe the statistics, you at least want to be fully briefed on how to keep yourself and your partner clean and safe. If you aren't comfortable with your family doctor, it's okay. Ask for referrals from gay friends.

Your Spouse

This is arguably the trickiest bit: a gay man concealing his true identity (or not fully understanding it yet) and getting married. If you have children, that's going to complicate it some more. Cases like these have been known to happen. Some work out and some don't. Remember, you took your marriage vows. While you are bound by it, don't fool around! Being gay is never an excuse, and sleeping around with someone of the same sex is still being unfaithful.

No matter how you romanticize the situation, a marriage boils down to intimacy and sexual intercourse. It is unfair to your spouse for you to withhold such affection. And it is unfair to you, to keep pretending and keeping up with a ruse. The best you can do is come clean, tell her what you want and ask her what she wants. If you have minor children, you should consider them as well. How will it affect them financially, emotionally, psychologically, etc.? Are they old enough to understand?

Your Church

On paper, most mainstream religions i.e. Catholic, Christian, Muslims, Jewish, Buddhism, etc., do not tolerate homosexuality. In reality, there are some churches that choose to look at other aspects of your life. Yes, there are Catholic churches that will not discriminate against known homosexual couples. But like them, you should make allowances i.e. no holding hands, no cross dressing, no make-up, etc., while inside the church and its immediate vicinity.

Personally, this is okay. You and your church meet halfway. How do you know what church is accepting or not accepting? Ask gay friends. Open up to a church pastor. Look at who belongs to the congregation, etc.

Be reasonable, if you want to belong and have the support system of your religious group, you should act appropriately and with lots of respect. There is a big difference between someone getting kicked out of the congregation because he is gay per se, as opposed to a gay person who lacks proper values and respect.

Chapter 4: Rebirth as Your True Self

The first 6 months after coming out are crucial. You want to dispel some of the fear that you're on a downward destructive spiral. You want to establish ground rules by which you and the people around you can operate within. As mentioned earlier, taking things one step at a time is a good strategy. Remember, you are in uncharted territory. Yes, you might have been gay all your life, but never in the open. Below are a few things to consider.

The People You Surround Yourself With

A new life means being open to new things. This eventually results in new friendships. Be very picky. In all the excitement and the urge to experiment, you might actually be pulling yourself down in the long run. Yes, you might have your family's support or grudging acceptance, but it can all turn to mush if you behave badly. It is okay to have friends who like to party and have fun. But don't forget about your day job, your old friends, your family, and the values you have been raised with. All must be in moderation. Learn to establish a persona that is fun, but not too accessible.

Also remember that you don't all of a sudden have to be friends with every gay person you come across. Just like when you were living as a heterosexual, you weren't friends with everyone; you were selective, and only chose to befriend those who fit well into your life and who upheld the same values and standards that you did. Keep the same standards now.

Stay in the Present

While it's okay to reminisce about the past, NOW is the moment to be. Concentrate on today only. In this regard, you had better be warned, you will have bad days; days you question your decision to come out; and days when you feel unsupported by others. Don't block out those instances. Yes, you should ignore inappropriate behavior, but you should also try to analyze what happened and why it happened. Also remember, everyone has bad days and good ones – remember you used to have bad days before coming out. This is a fact of life for almost everyone. It's normal. Keep your head held high, and know that tomorrow will bring a new day.

Look Forward to Something

The best thing to do is, end your day with a positive note, no matter how small, senseless or silly. And make it a point to look forward to tomorrow. I, for example, always end my day by treating myself to a little bit of dark chocolate. I also look forward to making friendly conversation with at least 1 stranger I meet at the subway station. Chatting with, and learning about new people makes me feel good, and therefore I make a conscious effort to think about it in advance and look forward to it.

Join a Parade or Celebratory Event

There are several mass demonstrations or marches held by gays and lesbians each year. One of the most popular is the "Coming Out Parade" held every October. Show support for your local chapter and bring along any interested family and friends!

Continue Doing the Things You Enjoy

So you've come out. It doesn't mean you should stop playing basketball, or baseball, or hockey, or whatever it is you enjoy doing. If anyone can't handle you being a guard, then it's their problem. Worst case scenario, you can join gay basketball clubs. There's plenty mind you!

Dating Rules Re-learned

Now that you are out in the open, dating will be different. If you already have a partner, then you are much freer to show your affection. Don't overdo it though. You are still expected to act under the same socially-accepted PDA (public display of affection) rules as other heterosexual couples—nothing more, nothing less.

If you are single, then being open with flirting with men can take some getting used to. Yes you are out but it doesn't mean you should be sleeping around with everybody. That's not typical gay behavior. Tip: take things slow. No need to rush!

Coming Out Never Ends

Yes, your friends and family members know you are gay. But the whole world does not, even if you do post in your social media page. Unless you cross dress, then you will have to keep telling people you are gay. This is a fact of gay life. Personally, I savor the moment I tell someone "I'm gay." I do it with pride and confidence. It's a regular affirmation and a way to educate the heterosexual population. Tip: you don't have to use it as a conversation starter. Slip it in the conversation at an appropriate time and place.

Dealing with Homophobes

There are plenty of people who like to bash the gay community. But I actually believe there are more people who now understand and accept, than who don't. That being said, bullies must not be tolerated. Ignore them if you must, but once they cross the line, do not hesitate to stand your ground and report them to the authorities.

Chapter 5: Ten Things to Remember

Dealing with Rejection

You need to know how to deal with rejection. Chances are a family member, a friend, your church, etc. might not accept you coming out as gay. Always bear in mind the following:

- There is always a chance at reconciliation. All you need to do is keep being out there.

- It is better to lose a friend or not be on speaking terms with a family member, than to lose yourself and who you are meant to be, day in and day out. This is what not-coming-out is. You will feel lost, without identity, and like a fraud. Over time, that only gets worse.

- Don't focus on what and who you will lose. Focus on what and who you will gain.

No Rights Given, No Rights Taken Away

Being gay does not give you special privileges to act trashy and/or irresponsibly. It also does not allow others to belittle you in any way. You have the same rights as any other person, and also the same duties!

Act Naturally

Act the way you want to, within reason. Coming out as a gay person does not mean you should cross dress. It doesn't mean you should talk loud and insert gay cliché words into your sentences. If it is natural for you to act effeminate and dress differently, go ahead. If it is natural for you to wear casual heterosexual clothing, that is also fine. By the way, you don't have to be fashion conscious or fashion forward. Just be you! It took a lot of guts to come out, so there is no need to pretend and act the way others expect you to!

Don't Be Overly Sensitive

There will be barbs and jokes thrown at the gay community. Just like there are barbs and jokes at ethnic groups, religion, blacks, Jews, whites, Asians, etc. You don't have to react to it. Assess the situation. Was it made in jest by friends to friends? Or was it said inappropriately or as a means to insult the gay community? In case of the former, take it as people fooling around. You can even laugh at the joke if it's funny. If it is the latter, don't take it! Walk away or say a few words to sober the group up. But don't be a kill-joy.

How to Deal with Kids

Chances are you have nieces and nephews. Act naturally but try to avoid swaying them one way or the other. For example: it's okay to bring your boyfriend along. It's even okay to hold hands while the kids are present. But it is never okay to tell them that gays are better off or superior, even in jest. Remember, you might think it's a joke, but it's the parents who will have to answer their kids' questions later on.

If the kids ask about homosexuality, well, you can answer truthfully. I prefer to discuss this with the parents first. It's not in any way censorship. It just prepares their parents for follow up questions.

How to Stay Clean

Let's be honest, you are either entering into, or being entered into, a place better known as an exit hole. So it is a good idea to consult a physician to know proper pre- and post- intimacy routines that will keep you clean, comfortable, and safe. More importantly it is a good idea to follow those instructions to the letter. Bear in mind, that any responsible heterosexual relationship also requires such a consultation.

Laws of Men

Gay relationships can get a little bit tricky, depending on where you live. Thankfully, some states and countries have already legalized gay marriage. This allows you to stabilize your finances in terms of sharing, inheritance, taxes, etc. In this regard, it would be wise to consider:

- Where you live: More and more states and countries are allowing gay marriages. Before settling in, why not research laws relevant to gay persons in your location. What is the status quo? What is it leaning towards, etc.? How is the neighborhood? Ask your realtor and visit the place. Look for crime statistics, etc.

- If you are not married to your partner, but believe your income or properties should be shared, then go to a law firm or accounting firm that can help you know your options i.e. business partnership, will, contracts, etc.

What if Someone Outs You?

Coming out of the closet should be your idea, your moment, your decision. But realistically speaking, sometimes you get "outed". What do you do then? Personally I believe you should not deny something that is true. This is because you are not only denying your true self, you are also making a liar out of someone who just stated something he/she saw, even though that person is nosy and should have minded his/her own business.

Gay Marriage

Like any heterosexual marriage, you do not enter into this lightly, half heartedly, or worst, drunk. It took decades to finally get a concession out of some states and countries to allow gay marriage. Don't spit on the faces of those who fought for this right by not respecting the sanctity of marriage.

Adoption

Realistically, in order to have children, a gay relationship between men requires adoption. The only thing you should remember is to do things legally. It's well and good that you want to become a surrogate for children of family members. But you should have things written in black and white, and approved by the state.

Never lie on your adoption document. This might not only lead to a denial, but also a blacklisting or worst, prosecution in an administrative, civil, and/or criminal case.

Never take adoption lightly. Make sure you have the financial capacity, ability to invest your time, and the go ahead of your partner. Tip: start with a plant. If you can keep a plat alive for a couple of months, then move up to a puppy or a cat. This allows you to gauge your capacity for emotional, financial, and time management. Of course this is true for heterosexuals as well.

Conclusion

Thank you again for taking the time to purchase this book!

I hope this book was able to help you to dig deep and accept the person you truly are. In turn this will give you the courage to declare to yourself, to your family and friends, and to the world, that you are a proud and responsible gay person.

The next step is to keep discovering yourself. Keep being a responsible and productive member of society, and keep supporting the gay community. Bear in mind that being gay is no different from being any other person. You will always be different, unique, and special. It is up to you to bring out the goodness in yourself and in others.

Thank you and good luck!

Oh also, if you enjoyed this book, please take the time to share your thoughts and post a review on Amazon. It'd be greatly appreciated!

Printed in Great Britain
by Amazon

16001947R00029